Turn Sabotage To Success

In Just 7 Easy Steps

Derek Chapman

Turn Sabotage To Success

In Just 7 Easy Steps

ISBN: 9798374107524

Derek Chapman

Copyright © 2023 Derek Chapman

All Rights Reserved.

First Printing: February 2023

DEDICATED TO MY DAD

This book is dedicated to my late father, Derrick Chapman, whose memory inspired me to write it. His passing has left a huge void in my life, but I couldn't have gotten this far without his influence.

I must also thank my partner Michael Angelo for spending many hours of his time typing and providing emotional support.

Thank you to both of them. Xx

Words about the Book

Derek Chapman is a consummate professional and first-class hypnotist. His Russian doll ⬚ technique breaks down change into the manageable steps required to avoid the usual resistance to change and facilitate new actions and choices.

This book is all you need to turn your inner saboteur into an enthusiastic cheerleader.

- Adam Michael Cox
Clinical Hypnotherapist
BA Psych Dip Hyp Accredited by the BSCH

Great work Derek!

I highly recommend Derek Chapman's book, "Turn Sabotage, To Success in Just 7 Easy Steps." Everyone experiences self-sabotage and his book will help you break the cycle!

I found his Russian Doll Technique to be highly empowering and I know you will too!

- Dr Steve G. Jones, Ed.D., Clinical Hypnotherapist

Derek is an amazing hypnotherapist who is able to cut through all "symptoms" to get to the real issue and then guide you to release all blocks in a way that is enlightening.

I highly recommend Derek to help you combat your sabotage through these 7 steps to emotional freedom and make the breakthrough you desire.

- Joseph Clough, Celebrity Hypnotherapist and Bestselling Hay House Author

Derek Chapman clearly explains how to overcome self-sabotage to make lasting changes in your life. He addresses common patterns of self-sabotaging behaviour such as remaining in a comfort zone, seeking the approval of others, and engaging in harmful coping mechanisms.

Derek shares techniques and methods for dealing with the contributing factors of anxiety and self-sabotage and offers a natural solution for overcoming these behaviours.

The book is partly based on the author's personal experiences and his passion for helping others change their lives shines through brilliantly. The techniques shared in the book are easy to use and can be applied by anyone. I have used his techniques in my own hypnotherapy practice yielding tremendous success for my clients and will continue to closely follow his work.

III

- Stephanie Conkle, Clinical Hypnotherapist

Why Read This Book

By reading this book, you can follow easy steps to make lasting changes in your life. Even if you have failed before, you can finally deal with those saboteurs that are holding you back from living your best life.

This book offers a unique way of changing how we sabotage ourselves. We all sabotage ourselves in some way on a daily basis. It could be from overeating; not exercising; drinking too much alcohol; taking drugs; bad relationships, or lack of confidence.

The book addresses how you sabotage yourself and shows you ways to combat it with an easy and simple solution, as well as a range of tips and methods to deal with the contributing factors of anxiety and self-sabotage.

Once you decide to start the process to *Turn Sabotage into Success in Just 7 Easy Steps* your life will become easier and more fulfilling.

I've spent a decade seeing over 8,000 clients just like you and showing them how they can easily and effectively change their lives.

This book gives you solutions to eliminate self-sabotaging behaviour and habits.

Resources For You

https://www.grimsbyhypnotherapy.co.uk/resources

Password: SUCCESS7

Table of Contents

Chapter 1

The Pain of Sabotage

Sabotage can affect us in many ways, such as feeling like a victim, being hyper-vigilant, being frightened to say no, or having to get everything perfect so we avoid making a mistake; and having to control everything. Avoiding certain situations, becoming bored or restless, and wanting to achieve everything as failure is not an option.

All the above can be triggers for anxiety, as for myself, Jason—whom you will meet later in the book—and many of my clients who were sabotaging themselves. The good news is that they can be overcome.

They say that bad news comes in threes. They weren't wrong.

I stood for a moment, trying to process the words.

"Your father has just six weeks left to live."

Forty-two days. One thousand and eight hours. I actually Googled it. Time suddenly stands still, and life takes on a new meaning. Just over a thousand hours to live. I kept telling myself his next birthday would be his last. No more Christmases. I'll never hear him sing "Happy Birthday" to me again. I felt lost, confused, angry, and sad.

My dad was one of the kindest men you could ever meet. I remember going to a supermarket with him once. He disappeared and, eventually, I saw him talking to a man collecting supermarket trolleys in the car park. They were both laughing.

"Where do you know him from, Dad?" I asked.

"I've never met him before in my life," he said. "He looked a bit fed up, so I thought I'd cheer him up."

That's the sort of man Dad was.

Oh, I could go on! My dad is my main inspiration. He's my biggest fan, and I'm his.

I kept hearing my voice in my head saying over and over again, "My daddy is dying. Daddy is dying, and there's nothing I can do."

How was I going cope? How could I still face seeing clients without crying or collapsing into a heap on the floor? All I wanted to do was curl up and go to sleep to escape these thoughts.

Looking back, it's strange how time stands still. I would check in and ask myself, *Did I really hear that correctly? Dad has only got six weeks to live? Maybe I was just imagining it. Maybe it's all a dream, and when I wake up everything will be fine.*

Nope! It's real!

The other patients at Dad's nursing home made the situation feel very real. I remember looking around the communal lounge, where around nine other patients from Dad's floor were sitting. They looked more severe, seeming to be further along with worse symptoms. One lady in her sixties kept shouting in a haunting voice, "Help me! Help me!" repeatedly, as if she were being attacked. This would happen hourly and was so regular you could set your watch by her. Her words echoed in my head long after visiting time had ended.

What I found more disturbing was seeing people younger than Dad being winched out of their beds while the staff changed their bedding. The real fear was seeing people being spoon-fed. I didn't know how I could cope if Dad got like that. He could still eat, walk, and talk even though he didn't know where he was or who his family were.

It was a traumatic time. A sobering experience. I just felt completely numb, and everyone acted as if it was all normal when we drank tea together. The patients used

3

plastic beakers in case they dropped them on the floor. They reminded me of those gaudy plastic beakers we used to have at infant school with their bright blue and traffic light red colouring.

The duty nurse told me that my father paced up and down the corridors after I'd left. He'd do it for hours, looking for me. That made us feel worse. There was no nice way of saying goodbye after our visits. He'd always ask if he could come with us. He'd have this doe-eyed expression that always tugged at my heartstrings.

In an almost lightbulb moment, I discovered something that allowed me to not only cope but to thrive. As a result, I became mentally stronger and more resourceful working with my clients.

I believe things happen for a reason. My dad passed away peacefully at 3.40 a.m., as predicted, six weeks to the day, on 24th July 2018. It was three days after his last ever birthday.

What I learned from that period gave me a unique insight. It offered strength, courage, and success to some of the most harrowing client cases that followed.

This book is about giving you, the reader, the same ability to *Turn Sabotage into Success* even when you're faced with extreme or difficult situations. You *can* succeed.

If this sounds like you, then maybe you're experiencing symptoms of self-sabotage. Some of the patterns of behaviours are:

- Remaining within your comfort zone
- Comparing yourself to others
- Striving to get the approval of others
- Causing friction with partners, family, companions, or coworkers
- Attempting to dominate others
- Engaging in dangerous practices (drinking too much alcohol, drug use, gambling, overspending, or promiscuity)

Do any of the above symptoms relate to you? If so, the first thing I'd like to share with you is:

- You can change because you were not born this way.
- You can *Turn Sabotage into Success* and be happy again.

By using the techniques in this book and making some changes, you will get through this.

Jason and many of my clients wanted a natural solution rather than taking pills.

Self-sabotage is a negative way of coping with life, perhaps borne out of early childhood experiences. The good news is you can change, and with the techniques

I'll be sharing with you in this book, you can begin the process of turning sabotage into success.

Perhaps even those who think that they can't change can create a new belief that they can.

Like myself, many of my clients sabotage themselves on a daily basis without realising.

How a Dying Man Found Life Again

Jason, in his late forties, was from Manchester with a heavy Mancunian accent. His skin appeared grey, and his eyes made him look like a rabbit caught in headlights. He was in the zone and not a good one.

I asked him two questions:

"Why are you here?" and "What would you like to accomplish?"

His voice started to quiver as he explained that he'd been diagnosed with terminal cancer the previous year and was given two years to live.

"I've only got twelve months to live," he told me, his voice growing higher and higher in pitch. Then he started to cry. "I don't want to die," he said. "I don't want to die."

I needed to break him out of this negative pattern. To shock him. If he took it the wrong way, this could go terribly wrong.

"You're not dead yet, are you?" I asked.

"No..."

"So I'm not talking to a dead person, am I?"

"No."

How I remained calm, I don't know, but I said: "In life, events happen for a reason. My dad recently passed from cancer, and if he was here now and I was getting distraught, I think he might say, 'I died. You didn't. Why are you getting so upset?'"

I explained to Jason that he could be suffering from the same condition I had. I call it P.O.M., and I experienced it often when I found out about my dad's diagnosis.

Jason asked me what P.O.M. was.

"It's called Poor Old Me!" I said.

This was the very first time I'd seen Jason laugh, and he *laughed*. It was a real privilege to witness. They say that laughter is the best form of medicine.

After that initial consultation and a few sessions later, his life began to change. He got all his affairs in order, bought a camper van, and went on holidays with his family. He adored his wife, children, and grandchildren, and he set about making happy memories with them.

He had a check-up a few weeks after our sessions, where his doctor was astounded to find that the Grade

4 tumour hadn't worsened. The most aggressive form of cancer, which usually spreads rapidly, had literally stopped growing. Jason's spirits were lifted.

He was eating better and going out for longer walks, and his wife and children thanked me.

"It's like we've got our dad back," they said.

Although he died, he was happier. He was at home with his family and had lived, really lived, for an extra six months.

I believe what doesn't kill you can make you stronger. Even though Jason and my father died, I recognised that I'd been sabotaging myself, which is something the majority of my clients had been doing, but in this instance, it was happening to me.

Throughout my training, we were taught, "You get what you focus on." And yet I didn't see it because I was so wrapped up in my own sadness.

Our minds change when we see things from a different point of view. The latest research shows that our minds are not static. By our minds, I mean that our thoughts can literally change just by thinking or feeling a different way.

The technical term is "neuroplasticity." The brain is literally "plastic," as opposed to years ago when we thought it was static like a sack of cement!

Many people sabotage their lives on a daily basis. When they see that for themselves, everything—and I mean everything—can change, as you have seen from the stories of Jason and my reaction to my father's situation.

In the absence of fear, we have optimism. Optimism gives us choice. With that choice, we can create new beliefs about how things can change. When we change our minds, we can change our lives.

This book is a result of the experiences I faced and my passion to help others change their lives. The following chapters will show you the techniques I use on a daily basis with my clients. They are simple to use and can be used by anyone, even children.

Flipping the pages and delving into the content of this book will help you better understand how to deal with anxiety and saboteurs. By completing the tasks and implementing the techniques, you can learn how to live your life more freely!

Chapter 2

The Cycle of Self-Sabotage

Every human being on the planet is self-sabotaging themselves in one way or another. It's a human condition. We judge other people and sometimes harshly, but what we're actually doing is judging ourselves.

Many people struggle against difficulties and despair, but their reactions and attitudes make all the difference in their ability to thrive. A recent survey of research on the subject of gratitude and its relationship to human prosperity during trying times shows that when individuals express gratitude in the face of adversity, they are more likely to use psychological strategies that help them cope and build resilience.

These strategies can include meaning-focused coping, positive reframing, elevating positive emotions, bolstering personal resources like perseverance, and strengthening social connections.

Anxiety is a form of sabotage which takes its toll when untreated. It can manifest in your life by not achieving what you want to achieve, avoiding situations, staying in your comfort zone, using alcohol and/or drugs, and gambling.

In order to change, we have to move out of our comfort zone, learn to like ourselves once more, take back control of dangerous practices, and respect ourselves.

When we have self-respect, the chances of self-sabotage diminish rapidly.

Let's continue my story about how I discovered a formula to assist me and my clients with self-sabotaging behaviours.

Although I'm trained in treating anxiety as a qualified hypnotherapist and an NLP master practitioner, I was unable to find a resolution for my own self-sabotage during my father's illness and subsequent death. Even though I used techniques with clients day to day, when it came to myself, I became stuck with a victim mindset of P.O.M. I kept reminiscing about my father and how much I was going to miss him. He was my biggest fan, and he made me feel confident because he was proud of me and encouraged me.

I had to find a way to work through this state of mind while still seeing clients and being able to assist them, which lead to me devising a formula I call The Russian Doll Technique, which I'll be sharing with you later in the book. Prior to using this formula with Jason, I had only used it with another hypnotherapist, Paul.

Paul, who was in his early fifties, kept revisiting in his mind a scenario in which he had caused a fire that set alight a telegraph pole which was connected to all the cables in his street. He was having sleepless nights, waking up in a cold sweat with panic attacks. Although Paul was determined to find a solution to his fear, he had challenges knowing how and what methods to use to help himself. He had tried various other techniques that simply didn't work. He hoped that, with time, it might just go away. After several months of feeling this way, Paul instantly felt better as a result of The Russian Doll Technique.

I wonder if you have found yourself in the same predicament Paul did, believing you may never find a solution to your issue. Most of the clients I see say they just want to feel normal and happy as they don't see themselves like everyone else. So I ask the client to calibrate where they are on a scale of 0 to 10, with 0 being completely overwhelmed and 10 with no anxiety.

The Saboteurs

As children, saboteurs serve as our protectors, ensuring we survive the real and imagined threats to our physical and emotional survival. By the time we are adults, we no longer need them, but they become invisible inhabitants of our mind.

Through neurological pathways in our brains, the thinking, feeling, and reacting patterns of our saboteurs get soft-coded. When these neural pathways are triggered, we are "hijacked" by our saboteurs and instantly feel, think, and act using their patterns.

For further details on the saboteurs, please visit https://www.grimsbyhypnotherapy.co.uk/resources

Ahead of their first session, I ask some of my clients to complete a saboteur assessment. There are two assessments: the first lists the percentage of how much they are sabotaging themselves on a daily basis, and the second lists their saboteurs.

The Saboteur Assessment

One way you can determine how you are sabotaging yourself is to visit this link:

https://www.grimsbyhypnotherapy.co.uk/resources/

I use this so clients can gain insight into the patterns of sabotage and how they are sabotaging themselves. This can then help determine the 7 steps required to *Turn Sabotage into Success.*

The 9 Saboteurs:

- **Avoider**

  The Avoider places a strong emphasis on what is positive and pleasant avoiding jobs and disputes that are challenging and unpleasant.

- **Controller**

  Anxiety-based need to be in charge and shape other people's behavior and circumstances to one's own will. When that isn't achievable, there's a lot of anxiety and impatience.

- **Hyper-Rational**

  Intense and complete concentration on the logical processing of all information, including relationships. Can be interpreted as being heartless, emotionless, or smug.

- **Hyper-Achiever**

  Dependent on ongoing accomplishments and performance for self-validation and respect. Recent success swiftly disregarded; more always needed.

- **Hyper-Vigilant**

  Constantly feeling extremely anxious about all the risks and potential negative outcomes. Never-ending vigilance.

- **Pleaser**

  Indirectly seeks approval and love by assisting, pleasing, saving, or flattering others. Loses sight of personal needs and hence is bitter.

- **Restless**

  Always looking for the next action to be more exciting or active all the time. Rarely at ease or satisfied with what is happening right now.

- **Stickler**

  An excessive need for organization and perfectionism. Anxious in their pursuit of perfection.

- **Victim**

  Volatile and emotional to attract attention and love. Strong concentration on inner feelings, especially unpleasant ones. Martyr tendencies.

Let's look at Corey, who was sabotaging himself 90 percent of the time without being conscious of it. An articulate young man in his early twenties, Corey had reached a point where his anxiety had completely overwhelmed him.

Although Corey was desperate to find help for his anxiety, he couldn't find a solution that worked for him. Corey had difficulty focusing at work. His only focus was his Xbox, but even his anxiety prevented him from interacting with other players, as he couldn't focus on what they were saying.

"I can't focus. I really hope this works. I've felt the way I do for years on end. I never feel like life is going to be happy and bright for me"—another belief that had stopped him from moving forward with a solution to his sabotaging behaviours.

These beliefs form part of the cycle of self-sabotage Corey found himself in all the time.

As part of Corey's transformation, he had to recognise that only he could ultimately make the changes required by seeing what his saboteurs were doing and how they were affecting his anxiety.

I wonder, perhaps, if you have found yourself in the same predicament as Corey. A number of my clients have, and they have seen how their anxiety is impacting their life and how they can change it by implementing the various techniques.

Corey completed his saboteur assessment which clearly showed him how he was being controlled by his saboteurs. Having a list of this on his phone reminded him how his actions were affecting his outcomes. Corey revisited the saboteur assessment just a few days later and noticed a difference in the sequence of his saboteurs which basically meant he was no longer victimizing himself.

In turn, this allowed him to feel more in control and positive about his future. This, coupled with my hypnosis audio file, which you can find the link to in Chapter 10, inspired him to get things into perspective so he could begin to break through the cycle of self-sabotage in a structured and focused way.

He would listen to the audio and use the 7/11 breathing technique, which is in Chapter 6, to further enhance his good feeling and positive outlook.

I asked Corey in his initial consultation what it was he wanted, not what he did not want. After giving it some consideration, he came up with a list:

- to be more motivated
- to be more confident
- to have better relationships with his partner and friends
- to be more focused
- to have a clear head
- to sleep better
- to be happy

Consider how you might want to feel. What might your list be?

The tools in the next chapter will help you understand and manage your saboteur thinking and anxiety so you can start living the way you desire.

Chapter 3

The 7 Steps to *Turn Sabotage into Success* and Overcome Anxiety

I've worked with thousands of clients over the last decade, and I've realised that there is a combination of strategies that can help prevent self-sabotage. Most people are sabotaging themselves in some way, either with habits of thoughts or habits of behaviour.

Underpinning those habits are beliefs that they can't change or are afraid to change. Every human being on the planet sabotages themselves in some way on a daily basis. When it forms part of our identity, we can fail to see it. People are often amazed at how good they quickly feel once they start using the methods and tools I'm teaching.

This book has activities for you to do and tools to apply. To get the most out of it, be focused and commit to doing the exercises.

Below are techniques to change how you feel and reduce anxiety caused by sabotaging behaviours. Each one of these will be explored more deeply in the subsequent chapters:

- Discover how powerful your imagination really is, looking at what our thoughts are doing to us and see through the illusion of our anxiety. See how easily we can delete and distort information and how we can keep ourselves stuck with the language we use with the F-files technique in Chapter 4, which will also look at the power of your imagination using the lemon experiment. You will see how your mind can influence your life both positively or negatively. Once you know how you want to feel, decide. Feel happier, comfortable, sleep better, and improve your feel-good factor with the grateful statements.

- Breathing is vital to our existence. When we breathe incorrectly, we can actually induce a panic attack. In Chapter 5, relax deeply with the 7/11 breathing technique, which is incredibly easy to use as well as highly effective. Lower stress with peripheral vision, which will allow your mind to become calm and clear. We will also look at a fifteen-second technique to instantly stop a panic attack!

- Improve your concentration, release anxiety, enhance confidence, and regain focus using the ball technique in Chapter 6—a great technique to restore balance and help overcome self-sabotage.

- Use your positive emotions to change any bad feelings or thoughts, even anxiety, with anchors in Chapter 7. Anchoring is a great technique and can be used for various anxiety-related conditions. They are used in The Russian Doll Technique.

- Tap into your own resources and enhance them so you can take back control in Chapter 8 using The Russian Doll Technique—a practical exercise to begin to reduce anxiety and self-sabotaging behaviours or habits.

- Examine how the techniques in this book have assisted a number of clients in Chapter 9 "Client Success Stories."

- Chapter 10 pulls together all the resources and is your go-to guide to achieve "The Joy of Success."

The 7 Steps to *Turn Sabotage into Success*

There are seven key factors that *Turn Sabotage into Success* and eliminate anxiety. By using these techniques, this book will help you gain control over the mental forces that lead to self-sabotage.

If you are sabotaging yourself with low moods or if you have completed the sabotage assessment and found yourself to be sabotaging yourself with any of the nine saboteurs, and their scores are high, you can work on them individually using The Russian Doll Technique, the ball technique, or the 7/11 breathing technique to reduce them and take back control.

The final chapters will help you consolidate all that you have learned and put the techniques into practice. Adapt and modify these strategies as needed to suit your individual goals. Remember, practice makes permanent!

We are all energy… the more energy you give these techniques, you will find yourself reaping the rewards very soon.

So now, are you ready to start your change?

Turn the page, and let's get started!

Chapter 4

The Power of Your Imagination

"The future is usually imagined as either better or worse
than the present.
If the imagined future is better, it gives you hope or
pleasurable anticipation.
If it is worse, it creates anxiety. Both are illusory."
— Eckhart Tolle

As in this famous quote from Eckhart Tolle, the mind cannot tell the difference between what is real and what is imagined. If the mind cannot distinguish between reality and imagination, can you see how we can sabotage ourselves quite easily?

If our imagination is vivid enough and we think it's real, we can use our imagination to create our perception of reality. This means we do not see things as they are; we see them as WE are.

Our imagination is so powerful because it influences everything we do, think about, and create—be it dreams, inventions, engineering, or the arts. Ultimately, imagination can influence anything we do.

We experience life through our five senses: sight, sound, touch, smell, and taste. They become the filters through which we make meaning in our world by seeing, hearing, and ultimately feeling it. Some people can imagine smells or even tastes associated with an event.

Our imagination generally refers to the ability to mentally represent sensations that are not physically present. For example, when you contemplate the lemon experiment below, you will be able to smell and taste the lemon without either seeing or physically tasting it, thus engaging in your imagination.

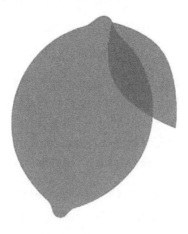

The Lemon Experiment

Can you remember the smell of a juicy, zesty, ripe lemon? Can you imagine what this lemon would look like? Unlike those supermarket mass-produced ones, this lemon is a big, fat, juicy Sicilian lemon with a thick bright yellow rind. This lemon's rind looks almost like a Seville orange, not because of the colour but because of the dimples. It's not perfectly formed. The taste of this juicy, succulent fruit is not bitter or sour—maybe because it's been ripened in the Mediterranean sun.

Using your memory, notice what happens… if you were to imagine rolling that lemon on a chopping board and applying pressure with the palm of your hand as if rolling it with a rolling pin. Now imagine what it would be like if you were to slice through that lemon with a sharp knife…

Perhaps you can remember an experience when you sliced a lemon in half, perhaps even hearing the knife as you carefully cut it, then noticing those two halves separate to reveal the moist translucent juicy flesh, seeing the white pithy outer edge. Maybe you can begin noticing those segments and the pips or the seeds staring back at you.

Become aware of the smell of the lemon juice that squirted on the chopping board and on the blade of your knife.

Some people might even begin to notice how their mouth is producing more saliva. When we have a full-on embodied experience, it can seem so real. By now or

25

even before, I would make a guess your mouth has been salivating more than usual, right?

Here's a video of the lemon experiment
https://www.grimsbyhypnotherapy.co.uk/resources

If you were fully engaged in this thought experiment, your mouth probably salivated. Perhaps you could smell the lemon or even taste it. In other words, you had a physical experience to something I suggested to you even though there was no chopping board, no knife, or no lemon!

You created this from the power of your imagination.

One part of us knows it's not real, but another part of us believes it's true. Similarly, when somebody has anxiety or phobic responses, we know that animals, blood, doctors, health, hospitals, insects, needles, people, and even methods of transportation can't make us feel anxious, but if part of us can have a physical reaction, just like the lemon that salivated in your mouth a few minutes ago, we believe our imagination to be real.

When we get this understanding, nothing can really make us feel anxious or sabotage us unless we buy into it because it's just a thought or a feeling. Unless we attach meaning to it, we are free, but when we get trapped in our thoughts, almost blindsided by them, then they always seem real.

We often get what we don't focus on because our minds tend to naturally process negatives. To explain this concept further...

The Blue Tree Metaphor

My logo is a blue tree. If I ask you:

"Whatever you do, DON'T think of a BLUE TREE," what do you think of?

Most of my clients, who really engage in that question, will say:

"A blue tree."

"Wow, how did you do that?" they will respond. Some might say a green tree or even a red tree which is fine. But they had to change it in their minds from a blue one to a green one or a red one first in a split second without consciously being aware of it. This just shows they have a quick mind.

As you go through this book, you will notice that all human experiences are composed of thoughts and emotions.

The average person has about 60,000 thoughts every day, which can range from joyful to melancholy. Our memories can shape our world—either in a constructive or destructive way. When we sabotage ourselves with anxiety, we often forget that it is an internal experience that we have control over; instead, we may blame external factors for our discomfort.

F–Files Experiment

As an example, here's how the mind can delete and distort our reality.

Can you count how many times the letter F appears in this paragraph?

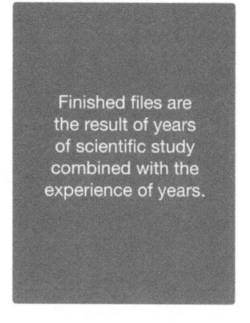

The answer is in Chapter 10. How many did you see?

Once we comprehend the fact that nothing can **truly** make us feel anxious unless we **choose to accept** it, **then** nothing can **have power over** us unless we **grant it** that **power.**

We create our experience of our world from the inside out with thoughts, emotions, and memories that can either sabotage us or give us a sense of freedom.

Consider anxiety when we fully get it. We know it's an inside job but we can forget, and blame things that makes us feel anxious. **Once we comprehend the fact** that nothing can **truly** make us feel anxious unless we **choose to accept** it, **then** nothing can **have power over** us unless we **grant it** that **power . . .** with the power of your imagination.

Reading this chapter will familiarise you with how powerful your imagination really is.If our imagination can believe negative self-talk, it can also believe positive self-talk.

Affirmations are a great way of reinforcing the positive changes you want and improving your self-talk. These have been written in a specific way to stop negation. In other words, you can literally program your mind for success.

Let's revisit Corey, who we met in Chapter 2. He was saying negative things to himself on a daily basis, such as, "I can't motivate myself," "I can't focus," "Everything is black," and "There is no hope."

I advised Corey to do the grateful statements/ affirmations daily for the next twenty-eight days while looking in a mirror and saying them with great energy, either out loud or in his mind.

If you use the grateful statements, you will begin to notice changes just like Corey did.

The Grateful Statements

If you say these statements and they begin with: "I AM THAT I AM," our minds will process it as fact. For instance, if you say:

"I AM THAT I AM GRATEFUL."

"I am that I am now taking back CONTROL of my life." It's UNQUESTIONABLE.

"I am that I am now GRATEFUL, and I notice areas of my life are getting BETTER AND BETTER."

"I am that I am finally DEALING with all my ISSUES."

Perhaps, "I am that I am FEELING BETTER within myself."

And "I am that I am now seeing the WORLD DIFFERENTLY."

You get the idea… so when it becomes a bit samey, change them for your own, so they're not predictable, they're not mantras.

Also, say it every time you see a mirror, including the rear-view mirror in your car, if you forget the bathroom one at night. Perhaps, even put a post-it note on your mirror to remind you.

I say to my clients, whenever you brush your teeth first thing in the morning and last thing at night, you can remember to say these three things:

"I LOVE YOU!" It may sound a bit cheesy, but if you cannot love yourself, how can anybody else?

"I FORGIVE YOU," so you are forgiving yourself for anything bad that you say to yourself throughout the day. (In other words, you are forgiving yourself before saying anything bad to yourself.)

"I THANK YOU," and you are actually congratulating yourself on what you've done.

Remove these words from your vocabulary:

TRY
CAN'T
HOPE

And after a while, this becomes second nature.

Make this a new habit.

We are replacing BAD THOUGHTS with GOOD ONES. Imagine how this is going to make you FEEL!

From now on, whenever you catch yourself saying anything negative, just FLIP IT for a positive.

You may begin to see improvements in your HEALTH and GENERAL WELL-BEING.

But don't take my word for it.

People will begin to notice this NEW YOU, and that will reinforce all the changes that have already taken place... and become even more PROFOUND... just like a snowball effect... getting bigger and bigger.

There is just no way of going back to how you were.

BREATHE and RELAX and just embrace this new you.

Always remember, FEAR is a False Emotion that Appears Real

F.E.A.R.

That's just it. It was just TRYING—and there's that word TRYING—to help you.

Let me know how well you progress.

Chapter 5

Find Your Instant Calm

As expressed in Chapter 4, the imagination can be an incredibly powerful tool. We tend to believe our thoughts, whether they are positive or negative. Many of my clients were able to replace their negative thoughts with positive ones using the grateful statements/affirmations technique.

One of the best ways of finding instant calm is to read the grateful statements on a regular basis and adapt them to fit your specific requirements. Say your grateful statements in the positive as if it is happening NOW. As in:

"I AM THAT I AM CALM."

"I AM THAT I AM SAFE."

You will probably notice after a short while of doing this exercise that your thinking will become more positive, and you will feel calmer.

Breathing

If you consider when we are stressed, our breathing is quite rapid. We breathe from the chest, and we imagine the worst-case scenarios which can lead to panic attacks. When we are not breathing correctly, we are taking in too much oxygen, which can cause us to feel:

- Giddiness
- Shortness of breath
- Heart palpitations
- Numbness
- Chest pains
- Clammy hands
- Difficulty in swallowing
- Tremors
- Sweating
- Weakness

15 Seconds to Stop a Panic Attack in its Tracks

The symptoms of hyperventilation can mimic a panic attack. The worst advice is to take long, slow, deep breaths because you're filling your lungs with more oxygen which will cause you to panic even more, and you'll starve your lungs of oxygen. The best thing to do is to **hold your breath for ten to fifteen seconds**. This may sound counterintuitive, but what this does is set the lungs back to normal functionality.

When you hold your breath for ten to fifteen seconds, your breathing will return to normal. This is similar to when passengers on an airplane are given a sick bag to breathe into because they're taking in too much oxygen. Inhaling from the bag resets the oxygen levels in the lungs.

Many people are not aware that they don't use the full extent of their lungs while breathing. Over the years, people develop shallower and less healthy breathing patterns, and this becomes a habit. It's important to know that the largest part of the lungs is located at the back, not the front. The 7/11 breathing technique's varied benefits include: strengthening the lungs; opening up the smaller airways; helping to see things as they really are; relieving tension and reducing worries; and improving concentration.

This proved highly effective for Corey, who had been so caught up in the cycle of self-sabotage he simply couldn't see a way out. By using the technique, he was able to remain calm in any situation, especially at work and with friends.

How does 7/11 breathing work? It does magic on the autonomic nervous system—when we breathe in, we get a burst of adrenalin, and when we breathe out, we relax. So when we make the outwards breath last longer than the inwards breath, we automatically send signals to the brain that we're calming down.

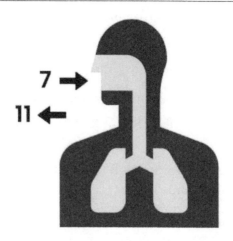

Find Instant Calm with the 7/11 Breathing Technique

Before you start, find a comfortable place to sit where you won't be disturbed and put your phone on silent.

Lower your shoulders by opening your mouth slightly, so you can release the tension in your jaw and shoulders.

Take a deep breath in, counting for seven seconds. (If you can't manage seven, do what you can.)

When you're ready, **SLOWLY** breathe out for a count of eleven. (If you can't manage eleven, do what you can as long as you exhale slightly longer.)

To make sure you do it correctly, on the out breath pretend there's a candle in front of you, but don't blow the candle out. This enables you to pace your breathing slowly so the imaginary candle just flickers.

Continue for five to ten minutes or longer if you can and enjoy the calming effect.

Tip to make the most of the exercise: Make sure you're doing deep diaphragmatic breathing rather than upper lung breathing.

A Fast Method for Stress-Relief Using Your Peripheral Vision

Are you in need of a fast and effective way to reduce your stress?

It's hard when you're in a meeting or giving a presentation and don't have time for long, drawn-out relaxation techniques. That's why I'd like to teach you about the benefits of accessing your peripheral vision. This is a method that can help you calm down quickly and easily.

I use this in my hypnotherapy practice with clients who need to relax. I also teach busy executives how to use it to get into the right frame of mind before a crucial event. In these situations, rather than going through a full progressive relaxation process or imagining a calming visualisation which can be time-consuming, this is very quick. My clients are all advised to make use of their peripheral vision because it calms people down rapidly.

Learning how to reduce stress by accessing your peripheral vision is easy:

Begin by looking at a spot in front of you just above your eye level on the wall. Gaze steadily at that spot while keeping your vision relaxed. It helps to loosen your jaw, so open your mouth slightly. This signals your body to release any built-up tension and allow yourself to feel more peaceful.

Without moving your eyes, keep focussed on a point in front of you while at the same time being aware of the clocks to your left and right (as per the diagram).

After a brief period of time, you'll find yourself paying more attention to what is on the fringes of your vision. Your awareness of what is around you, even behind you, will grow to the point where you can view more than 180 degrees.

As you stay in this state, your breathing will slow and become deeper, the muscles in your body becoming more relaxed.

When you're done, you only need to focus back into your normal field of vision to return to a relaxed state.

Why does peripheral vision work?

It's the opposite of tunnel vision when watching TV, using a computer, talking to someone, or reading. For instance, when driving, have you ever noticed that people tend to cut in and out of your lane more dangerously when you're feeling stressed? That's because stress results in a narrowed field of vision.

Enabling your peripheral vision expands your vision and activates your parasympathetic nervous system, which helps to relax and slow down the body. It brings your mind, body, and emotions back into equilibrium.

The parasympathetic system is responsible for the conservation and replenishment of energy by decreasing the heart rate and blood pressure, as well as aiding in digestion, the absorption of nutrients, and eliminating waste products.

It's also been found to reduce the amount of internal dialogue that many people have and can cut down on stress in situations such as public speaking or other scenarios.

However, please be aware that if you have any existing eye problems, it's advised to speak with a doctor or optician before trying this exercise.

Jane, a housewife in her fifties, was incredibly anxious; she was dreading the thought of visiting the hospital. She was tense, almost paralyzed with fear, and even taking a bus to get there made her uneasy. Her heavy breathing only made her more anxious, fuelling a vicious cycle.

Combining the 7/11 breathing technique with the peripheral vision technique, she was able to use this powerful method to enable her to go anywhere without feeling anxious.

Clients have reported that just doing this simple technique has allowed them to stop the negative chatter, see things more clearly, and get a perspective on life again.

Jane realised she'd been experiencing tunnel vision which had made her frightened. She had the added incentive to keep in peripheral vision when she left the house and encountered situations that had previously affected her. Because of this, she can now travel calmly, has created a better habit, and is no longer sabotaging herself by being hyper-vigilant.

Chapter 6

Enhance Confidence and Increase Your Focus

A lot of clients have racing thoughts. They are constantly overthinking, are kept awake at night with negative "head chatter" constantly asking themselves, "Why?"

"Why did this happen?"

"Why did that happen?"

Eventually, they become so stuck they end up hypnotized by the negative thoughts. The ball technique has been around for many years, and in various guises. I like to keep things simple because learning should be easy and fun!

The subconscious mind likes learning new things, so as you go through this technique, you will begin to find it can literally reset your mind in a good way.

Alice, a mother in her early thirties, knew her ability, but she was frightened of public speaking. Her new position meant she had to speak to a lot of different people, team members, and group Zoom calls around the world. Alice worried she would look stupid and become anxious in front of her peers. She knew the job inside out but was frightened to make a mistake and have people judge her.

This was affecting her sleep, her relationship with her boyfriend, and her general quality of life. She wasn't sure this simple technique could help.

After seeing the science behind it and how it uses both hemispheres of the brain, Alice was more engaged in the technique and was amazed at how easy it was to actually get rid of the fear. Just in a couple of minutes, it diminished, and several weeks later, she reported that she actually really enjoyed speaking to her team and got a standing ovation!

She did the technique as prescribed for twenty-eight days, and on the twenty-eighth day, she just imagined the ball in her mind as she was presenting. Along with the gratitude statements and the 7/11 breathing technique, which keep her grounded, she has developed a love of public speaking.

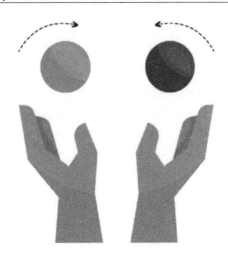

Enhance Confidence and Increase Focus with the Ball Technique

Just like Alice, if you feel stressed about an upcoming speech or presentation, apply this simple yet powerful ball technique, and you'll begin to notice how much calmer you'll become.

Remember, practice makes permanent!

The ball technique can be used to create a sense of relaxation, an increased attention span, a feeling that the problem is further away, lower anxiety, and increase confidence. The technique requires a ball or an object that can be passed back and forth between your hands.

Then think of something that's sabotaging you or making you anxious and recognise where it is in the body.

Rate the level on a scale of 0 to 10—0 being low and 10 being high.

Pass the object back and forth, starting with the left hand, while keeping the head still and centred as if held in a vice and looking at the hand holding the ball.

Do this for a minute, take a deep breath, and rate the level again. You might find it has reduced or disappeared due to activating both hemispheres.

Repeat ten times.

This technique helps to process troubling memories and troubling patterns of thinking, thus diminishing their negative impact and reducing self-sabotage. When we have an anxious thought or memory, and we focus on performing the ball technique, our anxiety is greatly reduced. Furthermore, this memory isn't as troubling in the future.

After twenty-eight days of practising this technique, you can do it without the ball even being there! If you are public speaking, for example, your mind has already programmed itself to deal with that sabotaging thought over the past twenty-eight days.

Jack retired in his early sixties. Golf was his passion and his life. He and his wife travelled around the world on golfing holidays to indulge in their shared love for the game. Until one day, when Jack missed an easy shot and lost his confidence.

Taking the saboteur assessment revealed Jack was a Hyper-Achiever, needing to get everything perfect which led him to engage in negative self-talk every time he messed up. Utilizing the ball technique helped him regain his focus, although it wasn't an immediate transformation as he had been practicing self-sabotaging for several months.

He found himself watching YouTube videos to improve his game, only furthering his obsession with the sport. At first, Jack was unconvinced that the technique would work, but he persisted and found that using the metaphor of a golf ball instead of a ball helped him to remain focused.

When he teed off twenty-eight days later, Jack also used the peripheral vision technique to stop himself from slipping back into his old negative habits.

The ball technique allowed him to find joy in golf again. He was so thrilled he took myself and my partner out for a meal.

Chapter 7

Replace Bad Feelings by Anchoring Good

Anchoring is a powerful tool you can use to reduce fear and worry, just like an anchor stabilizes a boat. We're all affected by anchors in our everyday lives without realizing it. These are formed through repetition and association.

You might recall the famous Pavlov experiment where he rang a bell at the same time he fed his dogs. Eventually, the bells alone were enough to make the dogs salivate.

This is called a positive association, as the bell was linked to a pleasant outcome.

Other positive associations can be:

Particular smells: fish and chips and freshly cut grass.

The sight of snowflakes descending taking us to good moments from our pasts.

These triggers also include touch, like petting a furry friend, and taste, like vinegar or garlic.

Unfortunately, sometimes anchors can also be linked to negative feelings. For example, if you used to date someone who wore a certain aftershave, and now when you encounter that smell on someone else, those painful memories come swirling back. This is an example of a negative anchor.

The good news is that anchors can work for you as well as against you; it's all about forming positive associations. So the next time you encounter something unpleasant in life, focus on finding something positive about it and make that your anchor.

Luke, a young man in his early thirties, had a terrible fear of flying. He'd been dealing with this fear for the past ten years, and it had become an anchor for his negative emotions. He'd get so anxious about the journey that he even resorted to getting intoxicated before boarding the plane.

Despite his deep-rooted fear, he was determined to be able to enjoy his holiday, so he replaced the negative anchor with a positive one. Through deep breathing and focusing on the positive aspects of flying, Luke was able to successfully travel and actually enjoy his flight.

Unfortunately, many of us can relate to Luke's experience of self-sabotage through these negative anchors. The fear of the unknown can take hold and cause us distress. However, by purposefully anchoring our minds to more positive thoughts and feelings, we can make it easier to both survive and even enjoy the journey.

Here's a quick tip on how to set an anchor to feel calm and safe.

How to Set an Anchor Quickly

Focus on creating a powerful state. You can do it with your eyes open or closed.

Recall the sensations and emotions that this state brings, both vividly and intensely.

To intensify these good feelings, squeeze your thumb and forefinger together for twenty seconds.

Open your eyes and think of something neutral, like popcorn popping to break the state.

To ensure this technique works, repeat the same motion with your thumb and forefinger again.

Rinse and repeat about five times! If the feeling isn't strong, repeat the process until just by squeezing your thumb and forefinger, you get the feeling back.

Test it. If you squeeze your thumb and forefinger, you will notice that the same good feelings will return.

During the 7/11 breathing or peripheral vision techniques, when your feeling of comfort or relaxation is at its peak, simply anchor the good feelings in. I recommend that you repeat this at least five times to fully install the anchor. If you're feeling stressed or anxious, simply squeeze the thumb and forefinger, and the good feelings will return.

Anchoring States

Here's an activity that will help you gain a better understanding of the power of anchors and reveal positive anchors that already exist in your life.

What words, tunes, or images make you feel warm and fuzzy or take you back to a happy memory? Maybe you think of a time when you felt powerful, loved, valued, and secure.

All these emotions can be anchored.

Take some time to explore and list them; it can be useful to know what resources are available to you.

1_____

2_____

3_____

4_____

5_____

How to Set an Anchor (in-depth)

Start by attaining a powerful emotional state, and you can do this with your eyes open or closed. Recall and savour the sensations and emotions that this state produces with both clarity and intensity. To make these feelings more intense, pinch your thumb and forefinger together for twenty seconds.

Open your eyes and think of something neutral to break this state—like popcorn popping.

When the feeling of comfort or relaxation reaches its peak, anchor the good feelings by squeezing your thumb and forefinger. It may be helpful to repeat this process at least five times to ensure the anchor is firmly embedded.

If you feel stress or anxiety, repeat the same thumb and forefinger exercise; you will notice the same positive emotions return. Test it for yourself! Squeeze your thumb and forefinger again; if the pleasant sensation returns, you have successfully installed an emotional anchor.

When to Use Anchors

Anchoring is a particularly useful tool in stressful situations such as job interviews, travel, or when feeling anxious. Anchoring can also be used in situations where one's habits or thoughts are sabotaging them.

When practicing 7/11 breathing, it's beneficial to use anchoring and store the feelings of calm you experienced. You can replicate these feelings of calm on demand with the anchor you have set up using your thumb and forefinger.

You can also use anchoring when using peripheral vision in order to etch in feelings of relaxation and calm.

In addition, you can use the anchors that you have previously listed to switch states.

In the following section of the book, we'll discuss a method that works with anchoring. Take some time to read up on anchoring so you can make the most of this powerful technique!

Chapter 8

Turn Sabotage into Success
Using The Russian Doll Technique

In the previous chapter, you learned how to use and set anchors to change your state. With the next technique, we'll also be using anchors as part of the process. The great thing about The Russian Doll Technique is that you can literally do it anywhere—all it requires is your imagination and focus.

I discovered this technique, and in Chapter 1, I explained how it was first used to cope with my father's illness and death. It uses the science mentioned by neuroscientist Dr. Joe Dispenza.

You can see his video here:
https://www.grimsbyhypnotherapy.co.uk/resources

He says:

"Who is in the driver's seat when we control our emotions or we respond to our emotions?

We know physiologically that . . . nerve cells that fire together wire together . . .

If you practice something over and over again . . . be it frustration, anger, or suffering on a daily basis . . . and that neuronet now has a long-term relationship with all those other nerve cells called an identity." (Our identity is just the "I am" statement we use as mentioned earlier; when we change our identity around our behaviour, only then can we fully change).

"We also know that nerve cells that don't fire together no longer wire together.

….. very time we interrupt the thought process that produces a chemical response in the body every time we interrupt it, those nerve cells that are connected to each other start breaking the long-term relationship.

When we start interrupting and observing, not by stimulus and response, and that automatic reaction, but by **observing the effects it takes** . . ." (Like in the large doll looking down at the tiny one), "then we are no longer the body-mind conscious, emotional person that's responding to its environment as if it is automatic."

The Russian Doll Technique encourages you to use all your senses to create a fully immersive experience. It encourages you to focus on your positive resources and allows you to turn sabotage into success or change a negative habit into a positive one.

You can also access my Russian Doll Technique via my resource page. Watching the video will show you how to do the technique for yourself—that way, you can practice the steps at your own pace.

How to do the Russian Doll Technique

Refer to the lemon experiment in Chapter 4 prior to doing this. Now ask yourself, after completing the lemon experiment, that if your mind is that powerful— that you imagined slicing an imaginary lemon, you imagined going into your kitchen, getting a knife, slicing the lemon, and were able to smell it, taste it, even salivate over it—can you imagine going into a tiny Russian doll?

First of all, think about something that's bothering you, something you want to change. It could be

you're feeling anxious or worried or that you want to change a habit, behaviour, or saboteur.

Think about the issue you want to change: How uncomfortable does that make you feel? 0 is not good. 10 is very good. Write the number down.

Find a place where you can stand in four different positions about a foot apart. (If you can't stand, use four different chairs.)

Ask yourself if you can imagine or visualise yourself inside a tiny Russian doll.

(Logically, we can't—just pretend you can. Remember when you were a child and how incredible your imagination was? For example, making tea at an imaginary tea party, which was probably cold water or using a pen as a space rocket).

1. Imagine yourself inside that tiny Russian doll. Close your eyes and double that feeling on a scale from 0 to 10, but not too much. If the number hasn't changed, repeat the step again. Only move to the next step when the level lowers. Now, assuming it's lower…

2. Open your eyes, step out of the doll to a **neutral spot,** then do something different with your body: **clap** your hands, move **around,** and **straighten your back. Think** of a time you felt **really** happy or content. Did you notice the difference and how quickly you can change your state?

3. Close your eyes and imagine you are stepping inside a medium-sized Russian doll, which is three times bigger than you. Focus on three events that made you feel confident, strong, happy, or unstoppable. Visualise each event and focus on what you can see, hear, and feel. When the good feelings peak, squeeze your thumb and index finger for 25 seconds to create a positive anchor. Open your eyes. You're looking for about 7–8 out of 10. If it's any lower, go back to enhance your resources using your imagination.

4. Now think of a giant Russian doll almost the size of the Empire State Building and imagine yourself inside it. Close your eyes and step inside. Notice all the space around you. Recall the positive images from the medium-sized Russian doll and imagine them projected in front of you on a massive multiplex screen. As these images play, make them bigger and bigger until you can step into them. Focus on the images for 25 seconds, anchoring the feeling of positivity before you open your eyes. You're looking for 10 out of 10, which is positive. If not, enhance your resources. Repeat step 4 until it's a 9 or 10.

5. From this large doll, look back to the tiny one. I remember thinking *I can't go back. It's like oil and water; they just don't mix!* Now, imagine that the issue you set out to address is the size of a grape underneath your foot. Close your eyes and grasp your anchor as you physically crush that grape with your foot. When it's

gone, open your eyes and notice the difference. It should have completely gone and you'll feel different.

6. Return to the medium Russian doll and imagine that half a grape represents the issue under your foot and close your eyes. Squeeze your anchor and physically crush that half a grape. Open your eyes, notice the difference, and see if you can get the old feeling back.

7. Now, go into the tiny Russian doll. Notice the difference, and imagine there is half a frozen pea under your foot, symbolizing that issue. Close your eyes as you squash that half a frozen pea while squeezing tightly onto your anchor. Open your eyes and pay attention to how you feel now. Can you recall that old feeling? Do you notice what's different now?

Paul was one of my clients we met in Chapter 2. He had found himself replaying a scenario in his mind, which led him to have panic attacks and sleepless nights—a cycle of self-sabotage. He was a very conscientious man who had carried so much guilt and blame which was starting to impact every area of his life. His first and only session had to be conducted via FaceTime on his mobile phone as he lived in a completely different part of the country and was in his work van at the time!·

This is where The Russian Doll Technique was a great solution for him. It was a quick way to get change without having to go too deep into detail or require lengthy conversations. Paul needed to deal with his fear urgently and, more importantly, was willing to commit to the process.

Combined with the limited space available as he was in a van, we worked through The Russian Doll Technique adding an anchor, which is detailed in Chapter 7, to crush the issue. As the technique requires four different positions, we were able to work around this by using the four available seats in his van—the three passenger seats and the driver seat.

Also, using the lemon experiment first explained in Chapter 4, we were able to hone his imagination and ultimately clear the replay of images in his mind and the associated guilt.

Ursula, a single mother in her forties, had moved to England to be with her partner of ten years. When she sought my assistance, she wanted to shed ten stone (140 pounds or 63.5 kilos). She was well-versed in the ways of weight loss: She had tried the Dukan diet, the Atkins diet, and the cabbage soup diet; she'd attempted intermittent fasting; she'd even gone as far as hypnosis and bariatric band surgery—but nothing worked.

Using The Russian Doll Technique helped Ursula remain focused and stay motivated. It also helped her change her association with food.

It is also helpful, while doing The Russian Doll Technique, to use the positive anchor in the medium or large Russian doll as it can reinforce the good feelings and negate the bad. You are only restricted by your own imagination☺.

Chapter 9

Client Success Stories

At this point in the book, you may have noticed that everyone's struggles with anxiety and self-sabotage are not the same. You can use the sabotage assessments as a guide to decide which approaches best fit your needs. As you take action, you'll be amazed at how much you can improve, as well as at the tiny changes that can make a big difference.

You might experience a stronger connection to your coworkers, more restful sleep, and fewer headaches or less tension. As you continue to use these techniques, you'll discover that confronting your saboteurs can be easier than expected.

The information in this book will let you better recognise the triggers for self-sabotage or anxiety. It will give you a jump start on preventing yourself from falling into familiar behaviour patterns. Understanding provides you with the tools to handle those situations as they come up.

How I Turned My Own Victim Sabotage into Success

In Chapter 1, I painfully recall the death of my father, an event that deeply challenged my confidence in the power of the mind that I use to help others. Despite the depths of my sorrow over losing him, I felt a sense of responsibility to continue my work and not break down in front of my clients. How could I help them navigate grief when I was right in the throes of it?

I eventually created The Russian Doll Technique, described in Chapter 8, as a way to step back from myself and view my sadness from a place of understanding. By seeing myself as a larger doll, I was able to remember the good times we shared and express gratitude for his presence in my life. Even though this was an emotionally charged moment for me, it was through gratitude that I found the strength to live on without him.

Let's go back to a few of the clients from the book— some of the many I've seen over the last decade who have been successful on their journey.

Jason

In Chapter 1, you were introduced to Jason and my own story, both dealing with the same persistent cycle of self-destructive thoughts and behaviors.

Let's take a closer look at Jason's story:

Jason, a self-employed businessman with two children, had been diagnosed with stage 4 cancer. Since then, his life had been thrown into chaos. Jason was constantly stuck in a loop of dreading his own mortality, which had emotional consequences for everything he did.

At times, his thinking caused him to worry so much that he stopped doing the everyday things he enjoyed, such as walking. He had difficulty sleeping and concentrating.

When we first met, I wanted to know what he wanted to achieve and what he was struggling with. Jason was hypnotising himself in a negative way. His fear of what was going to happen distorted his sense of living in the now. This let me identify the type of self-sabotaging cycle he was in, as well as any underlying worries or insecurities. To help him break out of this cycle, we devised his 7 steps to *Turn Sabotage into Success*:

1. Hypnosis: Learn to Relax audio file from Chapter 10.
2. The blue tree metaphor and F-files from Chapter 4.
3. The lemon experiment from Chapter 4.
4. The Russian Doll Technique from Chapter 8. Anchors from Chapter 7.
5. The 7/11 breathing and peripheral vision techniques from Chapter 5.

6. The ball technique from Chapter 6.
7. The grateful statements from Chapter 4.

Prior to the first session, Jason was given the Hypnosis: Learn to Relax audio file to help him relax, which he listened to every night.

At his first session, Jason discussed the impact of his diagnosis but also how, after listening to the MP3 every night, he was already able to sleep a lot easier.

Jason had been telling himself he was going to die. He pictured the worst-case scenarios and was scared of not being there for his family. By showing him the blue tree metaphor and the lemon experiment, Jason could see how he was influencing his situation in a negative way. We used The Russian Doll Technique to crush his saboteurs, which was key for Jason as he was in a constant cycle of self-sabotage.

After our first session, Jason said he was angry that he couldn't control his fate; by admitting that he didn't want to die, he'd created a mental picture of himself doing just that. I also showed him how by installing a positive anchor such as "I'm alive, and I'm safe, and all is well," he could train his mind to focus on the now instead of the future.

At his second session, we looked at how Jason was distorting his reality using the F-files, as we had already looked at the power of the imagination with the lemon experiment, which he enjoyed. It helped Jason see how he was not looking at the bigger picture. He had a loving family, people who cared about him, and he was alive.

By his third session, Jason was starting to re-engage with life again in a more positive way. He researched an organic diet, visited a herbalist, and consulted a nutritionist. He also enjoyed going out for walks once again, which lifted his spirits.

Jason was still hyperventilating at times, so the 7/11 breathing technique combined with peripheral vision, which was further enhanced by setting an anchor, meant that whenever he felt stressed, he could just squeeze the anchor and return to this calm space and tell himself, "All is well. I am safe."

At his final session, Jason revealed how his tumour had actually stopped growing, which astounded the doctors. He was still haunted by the image of his demise, and he used the ball technique whenever he felt overwhelmed. It would diminish the feeling, so it wouldn't have an impact on him. He admitted that from time to time he was still using negative statements, so by using the grateful statements, he could flip any negative to a positive.

Six months after his final session, Jason sadly passed away from his illness, but with the help of the techniques we worked on together, he was able to create lasting memories with his family and lead his final months with a mindset for living rather than dying.

Paul

We met Paul in Chapters 2 and 8. He was in his early fifties, married, and a hypnotherapist. Paul has been battling his trauma since an incident that caused him to lose sleep and spiral into a cycle of self-sabotage and anxiety. He was desperate to make progress, but he had no idea where to start.

Even though Paul is a hypnotherapist like myself, he was too close to the issue to be able to handle it himself. After a short conversation with him, it became clear that he had to confront his saboteurs before he could begin making progress. Paul's assessment revealed his top three saboteurs to be: the Pleaser, the Restless, and the Controller. This helped us determine Paul's individual 7 steps to *Turn Sabotage into Success*:

1. Hypnosis: Learn to Relax audio file from Chapter 10.
2. The blue tree metaphor from Chapter 4.
3. The lemon experiment from Chapter 4.
4. The Russian Doll Technique from Chapter 8.
5. Anchors into feeling calm from Chapter 7.
6. The 7/11 breathing technique from Chapter 5.
7. The ball technique from Chapter 6.

As Paul had only one session, we worked on a combined system of the blue tree and the lemon experiment to show him how powerful his thoughts could be, where he saw how he was sabotaging himself with his negative thinking and replaying of events. The lemon experiment demonstrated how he was conjuring up a feeling of fear in his chest and stomach. As one of his saboteurs was the Pleaser, the thought of upsetting anyone created a huge fear in him. He kept on replaying the negative movie in his mind of the fire and the neighbours complaining.

Using The Russian Doll Technique allowed Paul to literally crush those fears with his resources. As we only had the one session to work on this, all the techniques had to work together to reinforce the change, so an anchor was set to reinforce his resources.

We introduced 7/11 breathing to help Paul deal with the Restless saboteur.

The situation had constantly replayed in his mind, and in the weeks prior to seeing me, he had been stuck in a constant cycle of worry and fear. There was a certain amount of inner conflict with Paul; being a hypnotherapist made him feel he should have the solution; his Controller saboteur needed to regain his identity, but he was unable to control his own fear. The ball technique allowed Paul to minimise the images he was getting that made him fearful and helped him reinforce the fact that they were just in his imagination.

Immediately I could see by Paul's face that he had changed; he could no longer get the fear back. He tried in vain to get the feeling back and just laughed and was amazed at how quickly this process worked. In the following weeks, Paul kept me up to date with his progress; he was sleeping better, and the issue had literally gone. Paul was so impressed with The Russian Doll Technique that he not only bought the course but encouraged me to promote it.

Corey

Corey was my most recent client, whom we discussed in Chapters 2 and 4. A young man in his early twenties with a devoted girlfriend and a stable job who loved to play on his Xbox and connect with friends and family. Unfortunately, for the past three months, he'd been trapped in a cycle of despair, insecurity, and self-sabotage.

From our initial conversation in Chapter 2 and the saboteur assessment, we were able to create Corey's 7 Steps to *Turn Sabotage into Success*:

1. Hypnosis: Learn to Relax audio file from Chapter 10.
2. The blue tree metaphor from Chapter 4.
3. The lemon experiment from Chapter 4.
4. The Russian Doll Technique from Chapter 8. Anchors from Chapter 7.
5. The 7/11 breathing and peripheral vision techniques from Chapter 5.
6. The ball technique from Chapter 6.
7. The grateful statements from Chapter 4.

At his initial session, Corey used a lot of negatives, such as "What if it doesn't work?" and kept saying, "I find it hard to concentrate." We used the blue tree metaphor, which enabled Corey to recognise how his negative thoughts were creating his environment and mood. Coupled with this, the lemon technique taught him how to use his brain to create a feeling in his body so he could better detect the negative thinking patterns he was doing. Corey explained how he hated social situations and felt like he had social anxiety and depression, which is what concerned him most. With the Russian Doll Technique, he was able to increase his resources and reduce his three top Saboteurs: the Controller, Pleaser, and Stickler.

Following his first session, Corey started doubting if he could be hypnotized as he couldn't focus. However, after a few days of listening to the Hypnosis: Learn to Relax audio file, something changed: he was amazed to be able to relax when up until then, it had been almost impossible for him.

In the second session, we implemented an anchor to strengthen his good statements and sense of serenity to help him with his confidence. Corey found the 7/11 breathing method really useful in gaining control over his anxious thoughts. Through exercises such as the peripheral vision technique, he learned how to access a relaxed state after only two sessions.

He was also waiting for a diagnosis of ADHD, so we used grateful statements to replace his anxious thoughts with positive ones and embed them with an anchor. Corey hasn't finished all his sessions yet but has noticed dramatic improvements that have been noted by others. He plans to decrease his medication dosage as his anxiety has substantially decreased.

Jane

In Chapter 5, we were introduced to Jane, a housewife in her fifties with a lot to do and a demanding family. Jane's job as a bookkeeper had taught her the importance of accuracy and efficiency, and these values were often taken out of the office and into her home life. She was also anxious about getting sick and having to go to the hospital, causing her even more stress.

Below is Jane's 7-step strategy for turning *Sabotage into Success*:

1. Hypnosis: Learn to Relax audio file from Chapter 10.
2. The blue tree metaphor and F-files from Chapter 4.
3. The lemon experiment from Chapter 4.
4. The Russian Doll Technique from Chapter 8. Anchors from Chapter 7.
5. The 7/11 breathing and peripheral vision techniques from Chapter 5.
6. The ball technique from Chapter 6.
7. The grateful statements from Chapter 4.

At the initial meeting with Jane, we identified the possible origins of her anxiety. She felt confined as a child, and this followed her into stressful situations. She had been to many other therapists and felt hopeless in regard to improvement. Introducing her to the Hypnosis: Learn to Relax audio file enabled her to relax before her forthcoming sessions. She kept saying out loud, "I don't want to be anxious; I don't want to feel trapped."

By displaying the blue tree metaphor, she was able to recognise that she was making her fears a reality. When we conducted the lemon experiment, Jane realised that she was causing her physical responses by her thoughts.

During the next week, Jane continued to listen to the Hypnosis: Relax audio file each night, and it helped her greatly in reducing her nighttime anxieties. Her saboteur assessment results indicated that her most significant saboteurs were the Hyper-Vigilant, Victim, and Avoider. When she saw the results, she recognised how she was able to stay in control of herself rather than be ruled by her environment.

The following sessions introduced Jane to The Russian Doll Technique in order to bolster her resources so that she could remember her own power and potential. Being reminded of her accomplishments which she'd forgotten, and anchoring those resources enabled Jane to overcome the saboteur thinking that was dominating her decisions.

As a bookkeeper, Jane had a good eye for detail and an analytical mind. When she examined the F-files document from Chapter 4, she was confused by only seeing two Fs and completely missing the others. She couldn't believe it wasn't a trick. I showed her what else she was missing in her life that she couldn't grasp because it was so obvious.

Jane found it difficult to relax, but when we used 7/11 breathing, she allowed herself the opportunity to. Thanks to using peripheral vision, Jane was able to expand her mind by seeing more; the whole process enabled her to relax, and she commented:

"When I go into this state, it's as if I can notice more."

I reminded her that when people are hyper-vigilant, they typically cannot see the big picture and can find themselves with tunnel vision.

With the peripheral vision method, we established an anchor that enabled Jane to observe the whole of her situation. By doing so, her worries and irrational thoughts began to fade away. For example, one of Jane's greatest fears was hospitals. She had held this fear since she was a child. However, the ball technique allowed her to overcome it until even the associated images just vanished.

During her last session, we tailored grateful statements to fit Jane's specific situation. We encouraged her to recite them every morning and evening in front of a mirror, which helped to boost her confidence and reshape how she viewed herself and was viewed by others.

By the end of her sessions, Jane reported that she was now fearless enough to travel to hospitals and all other places.

Alice

We were introduced to Alice in the sixth chapter. She was in her early thirties, a mother of two, and had a hectic life at work. With a desire to feel more confident, Alice took on a new job role that involved performing multiple presentations, which left her feeling intimidated. Speaking in public was her biggest fear, and she was determined to defeat the internal saboteurs that were holding her back.

We worked on Alice's 7 steps to *Turn Sabotage into Success*:

1. Hypnosis: Learn to Relax audio file from Chapter 10.
2. The blue tree metaphor from Chapter 4.
3. The lemon experiment from Chapter 4.
4. The Russian Doll Technique from Chapter 8. Anchors from Chapter 7.
5. The 7/11 breathing and peripheral vision techniques from Chapter 5.
6. The ball technique from Chapter 6.
7. The grateful statements from Chapter 4.

When Alice initially talked about her new job, she was very intimidated about speaking with her peers. Her saboteur assessment revealed her three main saboteurs to be the Hyper-Vigilant, Avoider, and Pleaser. She felt like she wasn't worthy of the promotion and wasn't good enough.

Her husband was often away for work, leaving Alice feeling overwhelmed with her responsibilities. She'd often snap at her children, which then made her feel worse and caused her to reach for two large glasses of wine in the evenings as a way to relax. When I pointed out that this was actually exacerbating her anxiety, instead of helping it, Alice stopped her nightly drinking, opting instead for an occasional glass at the weekend. She replaced this habit with a nightly listen to the Hypnosis: Learn to Relax audio file, which really helped improve her sleep patterns.

The blue tree metaphor, the lemon experiment, and The Russian Doll Technique revealed to Alice that she'd been caught in an ongoing cycle of self-sabotage that triggered anxiety and low self-belief. By recognising this cycle, Alice was able to gain more confidence.

The week that followed, Alice was feeling better, yet the looming start date of her new job was still making her doubt her abilities. We used an anchor to anchor in her confidence and to learn how to say no without guilt, aiming to rebuff her Pleaser saboteur. The 7/11 breathing technique, along with peripheral vision and setting an anchor for calmness and confidence, helped her speak effectively and without discomfort, addressing her Hyper-Vigilant saboteur.

When it came time for her first presentation, Alice was able to imagine a ball as used in the ball technique in the room with her while she was speaking, which diminished her Avoider saboteur.

Alice beamed when she told me what she had achieved. All but gone was her anxiety; she had closer ties with her family, and most importantly, she'd grown comfortable speaking in public with confidence. Add that to the daily grateful statements she'd been practicing, and you could tell Alice finally felt like herself again.

Over the next few weeks, Alice happily reported back that not only had she done multiple presentations since then, but she was actually enjoying them! Her confidence skyrocketed and she started owning her identity.

Jack

We also met Jack in Chapter 6. Jack, a keen golf player in his early sixties, had been passionate about all things golf related until one day he missed an easy shot. This frustrated him because he was such a perfectionist that he kept reinforcing the fact that he'd missed the shot. He was contemplating quitting golf and cancelling his annual membership to his local golf club as he had lost the passion.

The saboteur assessment revealed his top three saboteurs were: the Pleaser, Hyper-Vigilant, and Stickler. Jack was constantly on edge regarding his performance and wanted to get everything right, even practising in his garden over and over for hours.

At his first session, we devised Jack's 7 steps to turn *Sabotage into Success*:

1. Hypnosis: Learn to Relax audio file from Chapter 10. 7/11 breathing technique from Chapter 5.
2. The blue tree metaphor from Chapter 4.
3. The lemon experiment from Chapter 4.
4. The Russian Doll Technique from Chapter 8.
5. Anchors from Chapter 7.
6. Peripheral vision from Chapter 5.
7. The ball technique from Chapter 6.

Jack had almost given up on golf completely due to negative thoughts. Utilizing the Hypnosis: Learn to Relax file and the 7/11 breathing technique helped him find a pattern of relaxation and focused breathing, calming his overthinking and helping him feel at ease when playing golf. He was looking at it from the perspective of the Stickler—having to be perfect and afraid of failure.

The blue tree metaphor showed him the damage his internal dialogue was causing him. The lemon experiment allowed him to recognise the self-sabotaging feelings of taking it too seriously. When he recognised he was ultimately beating himself up, Jack created an anchor that allowed him to stay calm when holding a golf club regardless of its material.

The Pleaser inside Jack caused him difficulties in sessions since he felt he had to please me, so this needed to be crushed. The Russian Doll Technique gave Jack a visualisation where he trusted himself when shooting a tricky shot into the hole, and there was no resistance. Combining this with an anchor created a two-fold solution: Jack could crush the Pleaser in him and learn to trust himself on the golf course.

Peripheral vision helped Jack keep his composure when a shot didn't go as planned. He used the ball technique every day—visualizing the ball as if it were a golf ball—and turning his fear of failure into something manageable and the associated stress into a nonissue. Six weeks later, Jack was enjoying his game more than ever.

Luke

We met Luke in Chapter 7, a young man in his thirties in a steady relationship. Luke is a high-flying poker player, having played tournaments in Las Vegas. He'd regularly travel for enjoyment, yet threatening to sabotage this was a debilitating fear of flying that had affected him for the past decade. His extreme anxiety about the journey led to him consuming alcohol before boarding the plane. He also wanted to reduce IBS and anxiety.

At our first session, we created Luke's 7 steps to turn *Sabotage into Success*:

1. Hypnosis: Learn to Relax audio file from Chapter 10.
2. The blue tree metaphor from Chapter 4.
3. The lemon experiment from Chapter 4.
4. The Russian Doll Technique from Chapter 8.
5. The anchor from Chapter 7.
6. Peripheral vision from Chapter 5.
7. The grateful statements from Chapter 4.

In order to get Luke's sabotaging thoughts under control and turn them into successes, we had to tackle any issues that caused resistance head-on. Opposing something will only lead to suffering. When Luke realized this, it made a massive difference.

His saboteur assessment revealed his three biggest saboteurs: the Hyper-Vigilant, Stickler, and Controller. These were causing the internal arguments which had impacted his sleep quality. By listening to the calming Hypnosis: Learn to Relax file every night, Luke was able to relax deeply and switch off the negative thoughts. His nightly routine became something of a positive ritual he never thought possible. Additionally, the blue tree metaphor demonstrated that Luke's "What if" thinking was manifesting his worries. He employed a lot of negative self-talk: "What if the plane crashes? What if I can't board the return flight?"

The lemon experiment helped him understand that his feelings were the results of his thoughts. He was able to make his fears feel very real, like the aircraft he was travelling on was going to crash.

He was great at going into hypnosis because he could focus and visualise easily.

During the second session, The Russian Doll Technique was used to show Luke how to view anxiety differently. As a poker player, he was used to taking risks—although calculated ones—but when it came to flying, he'd panic. The anchor for calm enabled him to use this technique whenever he was about to board a plane, and as he became calmer, he noticed his IBS symptoms drastically reducing.

Luke was having a hard time understanding the concept of his mind being separate from his being, but it was a good thing, and he felt like he had when he was 18 or 19. He started to observe changes during his last sessions. By entering a state of peripheral vision, he could remain relaxed on an airplane or during a poker game. Luke experienced a peaceful sensation as his logic overcame his self-sabotaging thoughts. We also explored the negative self-talk and changed it into positive statements with the grateful statements technique, which Luke adopted for himself.

Despite his fear, Luke was determined to enjoy his next trip and replaced the negative anchor with a positive one, emphasising deep breathing and the enjoyable parts of flying instead. He managed to travel and actually enjoyed the flight. He continues to use the grateful statements on a regular basis.

Ursula

Ursula, in her forties with one child, whom we first met in Chapter 8, is our final client. She had moved to England from Switzerland ten years before. Ursula was in a relationship that had grown more and more sour over time. This led to feelings of low self-esteem, anxiety, and depression, as well as an alarming weight gain.

Ursula's saboteur assessment results showed her top three saboteurs were the Pleaser, Controller, and Stickler.

We devised Ursula's 7 Steps to *Turn Sabotage into Success*:

1. Hypnosis: Learn to Relax audio file from Chapter 10.
2. The blue tree metaphor from Chapter 4.
3. The lemon experiment from Chapter 4.
4. The Russian Doll Technique from Chapter 8.
5. The anchor from Chapter 7.
6. Peripheral vision from Chapter 5.
7. The grateful statements from Chapter 4.

Ursula had found herself in a cycle of self-sabotage that had lasted almost ten years. At the point she came to me, she was ten stone overweight. Finding the reasons and triggers for Ursula's self-perpetuating feelings of low confidence and loneliness were key to eliminating her saboteurs.

In her first session, we used the blue tree metaphor to further show her how she was manifesting her negativity through her thoughts. Ursula's relationship played a big part in her feelings of worthlessness, and the daily responsibilities of her life meant she had little time for herself. Ursula used the lemon technique to help her see how she was linking her desire for freedom from her toxic relationship with her partner to freedom from her toxic relationship with food.

The second session focused on the internal saboteurs that were keeping Ursula stuck. She was naturally a very independent woman, and her life had changed dramatically since she had moved to England— somehow, she had lost sight of herself. The Russian Doll Technique gave her a chance to see herself from a new perspective and no longer be the Pleaser who would ultimately put everyone else's happiness before her own.

Ursula could consider her own needs without a feeling of guilt which also enabled her to deal with her own personal challenges in her home life. It also highlighted how she could use one of her saboteurs to her advantage. The Stickler meant that once she had committed to something, she wouldn't give up. She had committed to this toxic relationship, but she could switch that and commit to her weight loss. Ursula was able to use an anchor to reinforce her self-belief and momentum to remind her of her strength—the same strength she had when she first came to England.

Gradually, Ursula began to implement the changes in her life, finding balance between the demands of her relationship and her stepfamily. By using peripheral vision, she was able to see beyond the world she had lived in for the past ten years and see her potential. In the weeks during sessions, further personal changes occurred as Ursula reinforced her progress with the grateful statements, adapted in her own words for her own requirements.

Even though weight loss was mentioned as part of Ursula's program, it was really the triggers to her self-sabotage that were the core issue. Thanks to her 7 steps, she began to make progress.

In the eighteen months since her first session, Ursula lost half her body weight, and is finally happy. Ursula's weight loss was achieved through her own endeavours to dramatically change her diet and exercise routine. Her success story has even been featured in a women's magazine! Now she helps others select the right things to eat through her personalised diet plans. We work together; I change their minds while Ursula changes their palates—email ursula.aldrigo@gmail.com for more info!

By reading the success stories about the clients I've worked with over the past decade, I hope you're able to draw some similarities from them, which in turn will help you to look at your own circumstances and be able to develop your own 7 steps to *Turn Sabotage into Success.*

Chapter 10

The Joy of Success

Previously, we looked at success stories from clients that you encountered throughout the book. These are genuine stories from people who were able to work on their sabotaging behaviours and fears and live a fulfilling life again.

At the beginning of the book, I shared my own story about my father's death and how I used it as an opportunity to learn, grow, and help others. Gratitude was the key that allowed me to let go of suffering. It's now been four years since his passing, and I'm still able to think about him without feeling sorrowful. I feel blessed for being able to turn self-sabotage into success, not only for myself but also for others.

When you first picked up this book, you probably thought, *Is it possible to* **Turn Sabotage into Success in Just 7 Easy Steps?** In Chapter 1, we looked at how I was able to deal with the loss of my father, and Jason was able to confront his fears about death and live the remainder of his life in a place of enjoyment rather than fear.

When you have dealt with your self-sabotaging behaviours, it's important to work on your mind. We work on our bodies when we go to the gym, but we forget our minds. However, you CAN change how you feel, but you need to engage in all the exercises to actually change.

As you deal with your saboteurs, it's important to be aware of what you eat and drink and how you move, breathe, and think.

Why not make these a better habit?

As you seek out your own ways to achieve success free of self-defeating behavior and anxiety, keep in mind that practice makes permanent.

Consider the fact that our human experiences are primarily determined by what occurs within our minds. We build filters from past experiences and memories, especially when we feel unsafe; our decisions, attitudes, beliefs/values, and identity all shape how we view the world.

People worry from time to time, sending their nervous systems into overdrive. This can lead to rumination, more fear and doubt about our worries, and further anxiety and suffering. To resist the pain of these thoughts or feelings, humans will resort to any means necessary.

The famous psychiatrist Carl Jung once said, "Whatever we resist will persist."

So What's the Secret Formula for Success?

The techniques in this book work by enhancing your own resources and amplifying them will diminish the negative states. That's it.

I like to make things even easier because I believe the simplest things in life can yield the biggest results, just like the domino effect.

Our Experience, Amplified by Our Resources, Equals Success

My clients and I have experienced tremendous growth since we started practising the techniques outlined in this book. All of us have gone through a massive shift in our thinking and outlook on life. Some may be hesitant to accept the ideas presented here, but when they do, the results can be astounding.

The processes in this book are very straightforward, which makes it easier for people to gain a new understanding of the challenges they face—not necessarily why they experience those issues but how to find solutions.

Does the why even matter as long as you achieve progress?

People come to me because they've had enough of talking about their issues. They've had enough of reinforcing their identity by saying: "l abuse drugs, "I'm an alcoholic," "I'm a compulsive gambler," "I'm a smoker," "I'm deceitful," "I'm anxious," "I'm worried," "I'm scared," "I'm angry," "I'm sad," "I'm hurt," "I'm depressed," or "I'm guilty and too embarrassed to admit it."

Now they want to change how they feel. They're fed up with being the way they are and want to take action. They're exhausted from going in and out of rehab, spending thousands of pounds only to return to drinking or using drugs and feeling like a failure again. Or losing all their money and possessions through gambling, including relationships with their partners and children. It's then that we create a belief so strong that it can become unshakable.

Hypnosis does not require faith for it to work!

This book offers many success stories, such as Ursula, who has transformed her life and body and become a diet and nutrition expert, teaching her clients how they can also lose half their body weight while having fun.

By tackling your saboteurs and anxiety directly, lasting positive change can be made, which will firstly improve your relationship with yourself, and then those around you.

Finally, I would like to share with you a number of resources.

To gain access to the free audios and video resources, plus a range of bonus tips and techniques simply visit https://www.grimsbyhypnotherapy.co.uk/resources

Enter the pass code: SUCCESS7

Remember "Practice makes permanent."

I also offer a range of Hypnotherapy/Coaching Services for Therapists, Entrepreneurs all of which can be found at: www.dcmindcoach.com

Hypnosis: Learn to Relax audio file with instructions on how to get the most from it. Please read the instructions prior to listening. Remember, you only get out what to put in ☺.

Note: This audio file is not suitable if you have serious mental health conditions.

I welcome you to become a part of a growing community of 394 members! You can also access my YouTube channel: https://www.youtube.com/channel/UCPHUUK86Of DPuhsKlOTpTFQ, which features a range of techniques and testimonials, including some of the techniques from this book.

As well as a range of tips and techniques, I also offer a range of coaching services for other therapists, all of which can be found on my website.

Did you spot how many Fs were in the F-files in Chapter 4? If you spotted six, well done!

Remember, YOU GET WHAT YOU FOCUS ON. Why not focus on something GOOD? ☺

BE AWESOME!

Please keep in touch. I love hearing how the techniques in this book have helped turn your *Sabotage into Success*.

Derek

Printed in Great Britain
by Amazon

38326625R00059